CW00417932

Affliction of the Half Point

Nicole McMahon

ISBN: 9798651223053
Imprint: Independently published

This book is dedicated to my Mum, Dad & Dance Teachers without whom I would never have been able to dance.

***

Also, to my Brother, Danny, for inspiring me with his creativity. And my Sister, Charlene, for being my role model within dance.

***

And lastly to my cousin, Charley Farkins, for encouraging me to publish my writing.

~ 1 ~
Five, Six, Seven, Eight

The car ride was long, cramped and hot with four people travelling in a car, large as it was, it was filled to the brim with food, drink and all things tartan. Everyone was excited, happy and loud as my family normally were. My mum drove as my gran sat alongside speaking of normal life: their jobs, their partners and their friends. My sister would occasionally indulge by speaking of school, dancing and stories, just as conversations normally go. I would normally read and snack as we drove along mainland Scotland towards the glistening water. It felt as if we were off on a fabulous holiday with all the excitement and the occasional breakout musical moments of traditional Scottish songs. I paid very little attention to the adult conversation as teenagers commonly do. However, there was always a strange feeling creeping in the background though it hadn't got me yet so, I pushed that further down and gazed upon the Scotland I knew and loved with its billowing trees and unique mountainous landscapes. Even the busiest bypasses were not without their perfect views. As I stared out of the window, my mind would drift again to what awaited me beyond this simple car journey. My memories, dreams and experiences of the previous years set me up perfectly for what was to come. I thought about how not much had changed year to year but this year, I was wrong. It was so different in fact, that it deserved a book.

Occasionally I would catch my reflection. I realised at that moment, that this was probably the strangest thing about my relationship with Highland Dance. What the world saw and what I could see in the same facial expressions and comical words. I looked at the hair that, no matter how much hairspray and gel was applied, would never sit perfectly. It was then, I caught my sister looking at her phone and glanced at her hair, which probably had more fly-away hairs than literally anyone else in the world but to me, her hair looked perfect, remembering the green stripe that she had previously that she had to disguise for competitions, which had since disappeared.

Looking back at myself, I saw my large brown eyes, a boring colour really and quite uninteresting, however on further inspection, a sadness was detected with a slight fear and a longing to not let anybody down. My lips had turned up into a natural smile like I had just stopped laughing but the longer I looked, the more the smile faded. The light would reappear, and I would lose my reflection to the majestic sun, a sun that had stopped providing heat to this country long ago. I had begun being dragged back to reality and having stopped feeling sorry for myself, squinting, I looked towards our destination and there it was. The ferry port… Meaning we were nearing the end of the journey. After queuing for a short time, we drove up onto the ferry with the familiar 'dud dud' the tyres driving off the solid ground, ready to sail away.

Dunoon lay on the West Coast of Scotland and rested beautifully on the Holy Loch in which many a highland dancer travelled across every terrifying August. The hills looked majestic and the rain, which only seemed to come on as you sailed across the water, hit the loch like a breathtaking waterfall. How could such an amazing place be home to one of the most dreaded combination of championships in the competitive season? Onlookers saw such beauty and yet I was filled with dread. I felt stress, hatred and an overwhelming hunger to win. A hunger that, everybody knew including myself, could and would never be fulfilled. Truthfully, my thoughts and feelings towards this awful competitive homeland distracted me from appreciating the true scenic values and brilliant company it had to offer. As we sailed across the now rocky waters, I could see the small quaint town of Dunoon.

This was a place of glory, triumph and brilliance yet for me and so many others, it was true, heart pounding fear.

This was the Highland Dancing World Championships.

This was Cowal Highland Gathering.

~ 2 ~
The Warm-Up

On arriving at the house, we would start to unpack the car. We used to stay in caravans and lodges in the main campsite of Dunoon. There, you would normally neighbour at least thirty other dancing families at this time of year. I imagine at every other time of the year, because of the lack of dancers, it was cheaper but now, expensive probably didn't even cover it. Arriving to dance, chat, party, stress out and eventually celebrate or console with us. I was never sure why we changed from the campsite to the large house but it was stunning all the same. We shared it with my two dance teachers. Unpacking was my favourite part and I still to this day have no idea why. We would all help take the bags out of the car, but I was the one that sorted our lives for the next week into the cupboards and the closets provided. My mother and gran would sit on the porch with a drink and some snacks they had brought from home. If it was raining, the party was moved inside. Being amidst the hills and trees made reception a hard thing to find throughout the town but that made it better. Too many times we rely on the technology that we have bought ourselves or that we have got each other rather than appreciating the true uniqueness of the people, the family and friends around us.

I treated Dunoon as a holiday, a time to get away from whatever I thought was important when I was a teenager. When I was at home the important things were homework, parties, and if I would be accepted into the different cliques at school. Here none of that was important. In fact, Cowal Highland Gathering fell on the week after we all came off our summer holidays. So, after having two months off our learning establishments, we would ask for another week. Highland Dancing taught me so much more than school ever could. I would never be the person I am today without Highland Dancing and without the people I met through it. My relationship with my mum and my sister were probably stronger because of this too. With them, and my gran, I did many things in the countdown to the championship, but I cannot remember specifics. It was a mess of everything I loved, eating out, chatting the night away and most importantly spending time with those that we love.

I cannot recall if it was the Monday night or the Tuesday the year before that we had held a Christmas themed party. We invited our American, Canadian and Scottish friends from all over the Highland Dancing community to the house. There was a tree in the corner, artificial as it was, the whole scenario felt just like the real Christmas. It had been my job to decorate the tree earlier that afternoon with one of my dance teachers. Everyone else had went out to get last minute supplies. You may have thought that this was a calm and relaxing job, maybe even fun, however when the real Christmas came around in December each year and we got a real tree, none of us were allowed to touch it bar my dad. I never knew if this was because it was dangerous or because he was a perfectionist but what I did know is I had no idea how to decorate a tree. I think I tried so hard with this one to impress my dad of all people. He would not come to things like this, not because he wasn't supportive because he was the most supportive dad there ever was and ever will be. But asking him to spend a week in this confusing and loud Dancing world would have probably been torturous for him. Once I had carefully placed the tinsel, the lightbulbs, and all things Christmas on top of this beautiful green masterpiece, I stood back and appreciated my work. I was proud of this tree.

Later that night we had all been told to bring something for secret Santa. We hadn't picked names, we just put our hand in the bag and got what we got. I dressed as Santa, obviously, and projected for the room the famous Christmas tagline of 'Ho Ho Ho.' I had went round each person in the room until it was finally my turn to see what someone had got me. Then reaching my hand in, I grabbed the last item left. I unwrapped it as I did all presents, quickly and excited. I looked down at a silver Christmas ornament in the shape of the word Joy. This was the name of the person who had given this gift, maybe she wanted a part of her at your next Christmas celebration. However, of all the people that could have chosen it, I did. Me. Nicole Joy Neish McMahon. It really meant a lot and was hung proudly on our tree (with dad's express permission, of course) each year. The party must have went well that year as it became the talk of the town, well the talk of the Highland Dancing community. This year we were not doing Christmas. Halloween was this year's theme. My mum was, even though she will deny it, a fantastic seamstress, had made all our costumes. My sister was dressed as an Oompa Loompa, and not only that but she had persuaded mum to make her doll, Alice, the same costume. I was dressed as Morticia Addams, which later became amusing as I grew to look like her daughter, Wednesday. I can't remember who, but somebody had even brought a box of dress up things for any of our international friends who had not brought a Halloween costume for a trip to Scotland in August. How silly of them right? We dooked for apples, unsuccessfully and we decorated the same aforementioned tree with Halloween idols. The snacks, the drinks, and the conversation was flowing. Some of the best dancers in the world and the most esteemed teachers and judges were at that party but at that moment, none of that was important. Right now, we were just friends and I was getting along stupendously with everybody. None of us getting judged on our Dancing ability, just for who we were.

I'm sure most dancers had their own routines before the championship, especially one as important as Cowal. The day before the competitive task, they probably drank nothing but wheat grass juice, got an early night or they maybe had to do something strange like flick the light switch twelve times; one for every judge they hoped would place them. But me... I was different. The night before the Scottish Championship, which took place on the Thursday, I had my own routine of psyching myself out. Every moment of the day I would try to not think about dancing but after not too long my nerves would creep back out of the shadows. It didn't help that you could not walk four steps without bumping into another dancer, teacher or judge. Even the trophies that were going to be presented were in every shop window as you walked through the town. Some would say I needn't had been nervous, nobody expected that of me, Charlene McMahon's sister. I was the funny one, the one who didn't warmup, the one that didn't really care that much. But I did care. I would look at the program so many times before I went to sleep, so much so that the names became unrecognisable squiggles on the page, words that no longer meant anything. I did not do this to prepare myself or anything productive in fact. It was more of a reality check for me that, although Dunoon was actually quite a fun week, the dread of Cowal came from the knowledge of me not having a chance. The knowledge of not getting placed did not come from me thinking that the judges were not on my side and you heard that excuse a lot at every championship. No. It was because I wasn't naive, stupid or willing to believe in myself when I had thirteen years of evidence against me.

I wanted to tell these accounts of what I did, thought and felt for all of those dancers feeling the same way – that they're not good enough. And I'm not going to stand here and tell you that everybody is going to be a Highland Dancing champion because they're not. But what I can tell you is that it doesn't mean you have to quit. And it certainly doesn't mean you will never achieve anything because my name will never go down in history for being a world champion but anybody that knew me, knew that the little 'insignificant' accomplishments meant so much more as we shall explore together. Nothing to some other dancers but everything to me. I have never missed anything more than Highland Dancing and I don't think I ever will again. It taught me so much and it made me everything that I am today but could I go back? I used to say never but now, maybe.

Going to sleep on the Wednesday night wasn't the problem, it was waking up on the Thursday morning. As I said, we shared a house with my dance teachers but truthfully they would normally be gone by the time I dragged myself out of bed and into the living room, where my mum waited patiently drinking her coffee. I always had such respect for her. She never made me feel less superior than my sister like a lot of other people did. She acted like this day was just as important for me as it was to anyone else and I have never appreciated something more. I know people didn't mean to do it, comparing me to my sister, but it's too easy. My mum, and my dad, always made sure that I felt special and my sister never flaunted her success in front of me – actually if I hadn't got a medal or trophy at a competition she would happily supply me with one of hers. She was kind in that way.

I would sit in front of my gran's mirror, doing my hair. For years my mum and sister had to do my hair and make up or at least help but this time I wanted to do it myself. I think I just wanted to be by myself. Then my thoughts would get too much for me to handle. I would walk back through and just sit, listening to the casual conversation of unworried people. I looked at my sister as I watched her get ready. Her bun and make up probably didn't look perfect but to me, it was. Even the occasional wisp that accompanied her forehead would make me smile because it was still beautiful. I knew she was nervous and I also knew not to talk to her but she never looked nervous. Through personal experience, I didn't look too much at her or in her direction when something so important was at hand. The differences between my sister and I, especially here, was that she had a good chance of becoming Scottish Champion, of qualifying on Friday and maybe even placing in the worlds. Nobody ever expected me to be nervous. Why should I be? I wasn't up there as competition. To this day, I am still not sure what they saw me up there as but there was no threat of me beating them. I wasn't nobody to them, but they had more important things to focus on. The competition was a lot more important than friendships right now and that's what I was, a friend, not a competitor. This was a shame really because I was told time and time again that I calmed them, twice by two world champions in my age group. I made them, for one second, forget how stressed and how nervous they were. They just needed a little joke, a laugh or a bit of banter.

I was always known in the Dancing world but hiding in the shadow of my older sister, Charlene. She was a champion, she even held the title champion of champions for winning the most Championships in a year, she had actually won that three times in a row. She was amazing and nobody could doubt that, no matter how much I tried. The difficulty with having an older sibling in the same craft as you is people expect the same of you as they did from her. It's unfair how people are sometimes – them and their expectations. I couldn't really live up to that but hiding in somebody's shadow can become a cold and lonely place. They idolised her, little girls wanted to be her, and one even wrote an essay at school about how she was their idol. Charlene was as supportive as they came but every time she told me I had danced amazingly, she congratulated me or even gave me one of her medals because apparently, I deserved one that day, I didn't take it as a compliment, I just wanted to be more like her. She was so impressive, but I would always be the little sister, even though I was at least 4 inches taller and definitely two dress sizes larger. Feelings like that can really follow you even in everyday life. It can change you as a person. I started to compare myself to everybody, not just her and that is never a healthy move. There will always be people out there better than you, but that does not mean that you quit, or you lie down. It just means you should try so much harder.

I'm pretty sure that's why my dancing started to improve slowly over the years and then drastically when I hit the adult age group, when I turn 16. With every step I took on the path of improvement, I took one more step out of Charlene's shadow.

Slowly but definitely!

Although my sister was still so much better than I ever was and achieved much more than I even dare think about, I started to feel that I was slowly becoming recognised as Nicole McMahon, Highland Dancer and not Nicole, isn't that Charlene McMahon's sister? After a short while, I had stepped out of the shadow once and for all and into the spotlight where people could finally see me. No more cowering, no more hiding and no more avoidance. However, sometimes I wish that light hadn't been so bright. Even though I intended to stay there for a long time, being this much on display didn't come without its difficulties. My flaws were highlighted and everyone could see what I had seen for years. I had officially made a name for myself as a dancer this time, not just the class clown. I had never felt more nervous in my entire life, never felt so judged. My fake air of confidence, that I had relied on for years, was being slowly blown away in the strong breeze of this seaside town. And a new sensation was coming, something I have never felt before. Fear, I wanted to be better and worst of all, I wanted to win.

Still jealousy was a horrible thing and I was jealous of Charlene, everybody knew that. From her looks to her personality to a raw talent, she was the image of perfection in so many young dancer's eyes. She was good at everything and at first, I found that really hard to understand. I actually always worried when my friends were to meet her, they would realise that there was a much better version of me. Skinnier, longer hair and beautiful. Not to mention talented. However, it was then that I realised there were a lot of people better than me, not just her. I guess we all must get up, stare imperfection in the eye and smash that mirror down. Life is unfair, I learned that the hard way. But does that mean we ever give up, does that mean we ever stop doing something we absolutely adore and love?

Never.

~ 3 ~
First Position

We arrived on Thursday morning which was the Scottish Championship. Every single year, it seemed to get colder, wetter and more miserable. Yet everybody seemed happy. As the morning drifted into the afternoon, the drinking, eating, dancing, piping, and drumming became more prominent. All of these other people and yet somehow, I did feel alone. People spoke to me, a lot of people. My friends and family were there but still... A dash of loneliness seemed to crop up and blossom as the afternoon came upon us and it would soon be time for me to dance. I sometimes felt that some people didn't quite understand how it felt to not be a champion and still have to seem like they have the same, if not more, confidence than the champions that walked onto that stage with ease and grace, like this was just another local competition.

My teachers believed in me, my mum, my dad believed in me. My sister, three-time winner of the champion of champions title, believed in me and yet, I had never believed in myself. It was something that I was never able to do as a dancer. Actually, confidence in general had never been the easiest thing for me. I had no confidence in myself or what I did. But if we looked at the previous evidence why should I? They all saw something that clearly wasn't there and they tried to persuade me of it every dance class. It became tiring having to smile at everybody and pretend I was taking in everything that they were saying, although it was all lies. Even if I wanted to believe them, was I that gullible?

My dance teachers knew I struggled with Cowal and all the things surrounding it and they would always come to me separately and tell me the same things. Go for it…. You have nothing to lose… And so much you could prove. I would nod in a somewhat bored agreement, not because I was bored of them, they were amazing. My dance teachers gave me something nobody else could ever give me and I was lucky enough to have two. They gave me the potential to dream. Any dancer will tell you that dance teachers means so much to them in such a strange way. Like a mother, like an aunt, like a friend, and sometimes like a worst enemy. They were also the voice that you would hear every day of your life. Not just in dancing but I could sit in an English class or Maths, unsure of what to do and thinking I can't do this and I could hear their voice saying there is no such word as can't. The funny thing is I really do think they had faith in me but to this day I truly don't know why. However, I knew that they had many other dancers to get them the results and the trophies that they so rightly deserved. All I had to do was get up on that stage, dance and most importantly of all, I had to try. That's all we can ever do, is try your best and sometimes you never know, it could be enough.

Many people would warm up for hours before the championship but that wasn't me. I didn't want to be up on that stage where everybody could see me and my talent. Highland Dancing was a hard sport to attempt, let alone master and not one person could say they had won every championship in their competitive lifetime. It just didn't happen. Nobody could ever say that they had never made a mistake and every single judge from every single country and official board loved them because it just couldn't be true. There's so many different ways to do things in dance, so many judges with different likes and dislikes and so many dancers just as good and even better than you. Some judges focus on turnout, some on timing and some on performance. Even the world champions could and were bet. My dance teachers obviously wanted me to do well, and they always had a strange feeling that I had all this talent but hadn't shown it yet. That I had all this wasted potential. It was kind of them but where they saw all of it, I would never know. However, I nodded to them as I held in the disbelieving laughter that wanted to burst out. I guess I thought they wouldn't understand if I told them why I didn't practise every day and why I didn't want to improve. See, I liked having an excuse as to why I did so badly against the champions. I guess if I improved my fitness or I practised every day, it would become harder to accept defeat and loss. Every trophy that past my hands to another dancer, would've killed me. But even when and if I had wanted to improve, it was hard to find that willpower to keep going after the results at each competition. It was the very first catch 22 in my young life. It's hard when you know you can't beat the dancers that turn up to the smaller competitions and so I had to ask myself how to beat those champions who are battling it out for the world title? The one good thing about being Scottish at the Cowal Highland Gathering, was that we could compete on the Thursday for the Scottish Championship. Nowadays a lot of dancers, Scottish dancers, won't compete on the Thursday. See, if you qualify on Friday then you'll have to do another championship on the Saturday to battle for the world championship title. A lot of dancers see it in their best interest not to tire themselves out on the Thursday which would've been brilliant for me however this fad started to take place as I was leaving the dancing world, so I wasn't so fortunate to have those champions take a break that day.

When it was time to get into my kilt and start that dreaded warmup, I had to be alone for a bit as too many people had too much to say. However, not for too long either… Too long would have made me start questioning why I was there and if there is even a point in getting up on that stage. Every year at this exact moment, I wanted to run.

Before I danced, I had to watch so many champion dancers, my friends, walk up and perform. In Highland Dancing, the quicker your entry for the competition or the championship is posted, the later you will dance in the age group. Most dancers battle it out for who can dance last, who can stay in the judge's mind the longest and the latest. And my mum did do this for my sister. She used to do it for me. But a few years previous, I'd asked her to stop. I didn't want to watch brilliant dancers go on before me. I also didn't want to be on stage at the same time as those amazing dancers and be compared right next to them. Neither did I want to be right at the start. This had nothing to do with my mental capacity, if anything, it had to do with my physical capacity as I didn't want to volunteer for a Reel which needed four dancers. If the group was not big enough, the first three were called on in the group to dance again and that was too much for me. The dancers in my group were obviously my age but so much more experienced. If anything, I may have done more competitions than them, or I may have danced longer than them as I started dancing at three years old. However they looked better. Then I would have to watch as the crowd applauded and cheered them on. They all had a look of confidence about them that said, Watch Me. Place Me. Give Me the Trophy. When I went up there I had to dance like I was a champion on that grand wooden platform when I knew fine well I was worth less than the dusty footprints the previous dancers had left behind. These dancers knew exactly what they were doing and why they were doing it.. Their technique was almost flawless and most of all, they were at the prime of their fitness. When they were warming up nervously beside me, some of them looked petrified but something must happened in the time it took them to walk onto the boards because when they danced... Wow. When they danced, they were different people. There were no longer my friends, there was no doubting it, these girls were performers. They looked like moving statues, so perfect that they could only be the work of an artist that should be admired for years. Their figures perfect, their make up flawless and the way their bodies moved and their kilt wrapped around them was incredible. I could watch them for hours and still never find an imperfection. Yet, they could glance at me for a mere second and see everything that was wrong. They were dancers. I wasn't as good and I didn't win as many Championships but even after saying all this, I was a dancer too and I was going to prove it.

I stood on the boards jumping up and down, not practising just trying to keep moving in the freezing cold, wishing the next to dance good luck, or in the Dancing world, break a leg and offering a heartfelt well done to anybody coming off, panting heavily. I loved walking off, I always had his newfound appreciation for Scottish weather. It cooled me down completely taking away the burning feeling of breathlessness in my throat and wiped away the sweat rolling down the back of my jacket onto my back. But soon became my turn to go through that high archway, up those soul-destroying steps and onto that dreaded raised platform that hadn't even been there days before.

~ 4 ~
Highland Fling

Feeling the wind on my face whilst I stood there shaking, whether I was shaking because it was so cold or through nerves I may never know. The judges nodded in unison to allow the four dancers who had just finished walk off stage. They turned to their right and from the corner of their mouth, they said good luck. My automatic reaction, actually any dancer's automatic reaction in this situation was to say well done without moving your lips, accompanied by the faintest trace of a smile. I looked down towards the three judges who had a small covering over their chairs and tables, but as I saw their judge's papers slightly flapping, I knew it wasn't completely windproof. I saw them glance at me following the three dancers to my right, they may have just wrote the number on my kilt down as a formality. Very much doubt any of them had any intention of awarding me enough marks to place me in the lineup, but I'm not blaming them. There were brilliant champions in this age group. Some dancers have a little bit of luck. Their birthdays fell on the right day, their main competitors weren't in their age group for the full year. This was a great group all year round... Sadly.

I looked out towards the hundreds of people staring at the spot in which I stood. They were all thinking the same thing when watching Highland Dancing. Who was dancing well, who had a chance here, who was going to win, and who was going to be greatly disappointed that year? Yet I didn't care about any of them and I can't imagine many of them cared about watching me. Could they even see me? I always looked for my mum, my sister and one of my dance teachers in the vast crowds and always found them almost immediately. Sometimes I couldn't look at the seat in which they were sitting because they have just had to run from another dancer on another platform but they always made it to see me dance. My mum looked proud, excited and happy. My sister look nervous, maybe for me, maybe for herself, but probably for both of us. However, I always needed to find them; they were the people I was dancing for. They were the people I was performing to. Their opinions of me meant so much, in fact they meant everything. I looked away from them, trying not to distract myself. I found a spot to focus on. There were numbers right in front of us above the chairs, above the seating, above the politics. I would stare intensely at that number, it lifted my chin, it made me relax and it made me realise this was it. I had to dance. I stared so intensely, through the rain and into the place that was not true, that was not there. Into the place where everybody was watching me. Into the place where I was the world champion and there were no real worries or concerns. I always had to come here when I was dancing. It helped. I had imagined I was the one everybody had come to see.

I stood in first position, ready to go – forcing my heels together as my calves solidly tried to push them apart. Then the skilful tune of the bagpiping began. I began the Highland Fling and so many different things raced through my head. But over and over again, I thought I had to dance. Really dance. I had to say Watch me. Place me. Give me the trophy. So many moments can rush through your head in a split second, so many memories but

I had just one. In the memory that flashed, all I saw was me Dancing this very dance but I was almost 100 miles away, in a gymnasium hall with only two other girls beside me and every single eye was on us. There were three judges in front of us and my mum, my sister, my northern Irish family and my dance school were watching to my right. Some of the most respected people in Highland dance watched me from the tables and door behind me, the three tables in front of me and the crowd beyond. That is all I saw in a split second but it meant so much to me. This had happened at a Musselburgh Championship, the August before. The championship was named the East of Scotland and it was my qualifier for the Area Finals that took place in late April/early May. There were three dance schools with one student from each that all got the same amount of points during this championship. But we needed a winner, not of the championship, no, but to be the reserve on the area finals adult team. This was a very rare occurrence. In actuality I don't remember of another time that this happened. But, it was like the movies, this was a dance off. I was excited, nervous and a little annoyed that I had to do another dance. My sister had taken me aside not 15 minutes earlier, and gave me the greatest pep-talk anyone has ever given me to this day. I can't even remember what was said exactly but she had the purest of words and an uncontaminated belief in me. For once I really did have a chance. I put my jacket on, rolled my socks up, took to the floor and I danced with absolutely everything I could possibly give. I got to the last step and I had used every single part of myself I possibly had but I looked into the audience and I could see people watching me. I got every single little ounce of energy I possibly had and did not quit. So much so that as a bowed I feared I may never have been able to stand back up. As I exited the stage, I felt my legs were shaking and my arms were weak. I almost collapsed on the floor next to my peers, next to the dance school that I, myself, had just been the face of. I have never in my life been so sure I was going to win something. The results came and they announced the under 12 years results. They did the same for the under 16 years, announcing first to sixth, then the two qualifying dancers of the age group and lastly the reserve for that age group. It came to the adults. First to sixth was announced, and the two qualifying dancers for that age group. At this point you could cut the tension in the hall with a knife. Nobody seemed to be looking at each other yet everybody was looking at everyone. I have never done this in my life but I got ready to accept my award that I did not know I had yet. Luckily I hadn't stood up.

As the reserve went to somebody else.

I found out later on, that of the three judges and the three dancers I got placed third by two of them and second by one of them. Out of the three girls I had come last. I had never been confident before but if anything had shattered my confidence in Highland Dancing concerning my ability, it was that moment and to this day when I speak of it, I cry.

This flashback moment was quick as I stood there listening to that familiar tune of the Highland Fling. I looked back into the crowd, letting my attention slip for a millisecond to see if people were looking at me the same way as they did back then but nobody was looking, not at me. The few people that were looking were all that was important. The thing with people is they will always see the fake smile spread across your face but they will never see the tears in her eyes or the sadness in your gaze because people look but they never really see. They never see what they don't want to, what would make them uncomfortable. But I still danced with everything I had. Since that Fling in Musselburgh, I had pushed myself every time I danced. Sometimes I had more to give than others but today I had a lot to give and I knew in that moment today was going to be sore. And until a dancer can feel pain to the extent they don't know if it's tears or sweat that has started to cloud their vision and yet they keep going and in fact dance harder, dance more and dance better than ever before, until then a person cannot really call themselves a Highland Dancer. However, when that final bow at the end of your dance is complete and the drones from the pipes die out, you can only feel one of two things. Complete regret as you know you could've danced so much better or you could get what

I felt at the end of my fling, back in Musselburgh on that dreaded day and in that moment, on that platform, on that Thursday at Cowal. Complete happiness and I was proud of myself and as I let my eyes look back at my mum and my sister, I knew they were proud too. One of the four dances was complete. I had done it to the best of my ability and I had finally proven to myself that Nicole McMahon was moving up in the Dancing world. I would never reach the top of the ladder but I climbed higher that day. My Fling had told people to watch me. Place me. Give me the trophy. Even if they didn't listen, I had shouted and I had got somebody's attention. Yes, people like me may never have won these things, might never have won one of these championships or titles. But people like me made a statement and I refused and still refuse to let the dancing world forget who I was.

~ 5 ~
Swords

Once the first dance was complete, you would think I would start to destress. However, nobody could really be calm before the Swords. In a championship like Cowal there does seem to be a long wait between dances because of the amount of terrific dancers that show up every year. I spent this time talking. It was an amazing opportunity to be somewhere like this, an opportunity that some of us take for granted. Not many people get to speak to someone from Texas in the same conversation as someone from Edinburgh, someone from Ontario and someone from California at the same time about a subject that we were all interested in. It's quite surreal. Now was my favourite time to not think about what I was going to have to do, if I had been old enough for a drink, I feel like this would've been the perfect time for some Dutch courage but then again it was hard enough to dance over one set of Swords, without seeing double. It was still chilly, and the sweat and heat my body had produced from the Highland Fling, was no longer enough to keep me warm. We complain a lot about the weather in Scotland but at a time like this it was best that the Sun wasn't out. I would dance and be exhausted enough without a headache, occurring because I had to squint through the Sun.

With regards to telling Highland Dancing stories, I have many. But when it came to the Swords I had very few. The Swords is very much, are you going to kick them, or not? I've failed many times in the Swords. I've collapsed onto them, I've landed, bum first, onto the hilt (giving me a colour changing bruise that lasted for weeks), and I've done some amazing Swords. The main thing you've got to have with the Swords is a good half point. Anyone out there that dances, knows the affliction of the half point. It's too easy to pretend to do one and not put weight on it, it's too easy to let it slide down into a ball position, because life is easier when we take shortcuts and it's true. But it's not right. I've always thought a good half point separated the good dancers from the great. Mine was never strong, I cheated many a time and my highcuts were never extended but my body angles were always good as they had been drilled into our heads. My fitness wasn't good enough for a Swords, the most energy exertion is in the first step and you still had three to go. You can't sit on a movement or it will take so much more energy to get back up, again a shortcut we think will work. But that clap going into the last step, gave me energy. Which was sometimes a struggle if there were two last steps and only one clap. It is at this time that I would bring a clap for every last step in. Its like your uncle hitting his knee when it was time to leave. It gave him the energy to stand up off the couch that had enveloped him for hours.

Not many people's favourite dance was the Swords. And those whose it was, I can only imagine they still worried about kicking it. When I embarked on the Swords this day, and climbed onto the stage, I was nervous. The one dance that no matter how well you do, you could still kick them and lose. A traditional Highland Dancing ritual was once the dancers, that had danced before you, walked off the stage you had to fix your Swords to the perfect angles for yourself. The way I fixed them was so that the one space between the hilts, what I would call the danger zone, was the biggest. It made me feel slightly more optimistic.

The pipes began as they always do, the tune was motivating and although repetitive, it was actually one of my favourites. Apparently when I was a child, and my mum took me to competitions for my sister, I would fall asleep in the pram to this song. I'd give anything to be back in that pram. My teachers and my mum's notes came through my head at that moment. One of my dance teachers would have said head up, shoulders down and remember two beat pas-de-basques. My other dance teacher would've said body angles, elevation and remember two beat pas-de-basques and my mum would say remember two beat pas-de-basques. As I bowed and raised onto the balls of both feet, I extended my leg to the right to begin my first pas-de-basque, I thought about all of those notes and tried to take them onboard. As I sprang onto my right foot, taking my left foot into third, I realised what I had just done... A three-beat pas-de-basque. If you did this all the way round the Swords, you could've actually got disqualified for being out of time. Technically you're doing the wrong timing for the dance but luckily after noticing that, the rest of them were fine, the highcuts not so much. As I jumped into the Swords, my head went down. The one Highland dance you're allowed to look down as a dancer and I didn't like it. It made the dance look like a mere combination of movements and not a performance. Plus when your head went down, your arms came down, your back arches, and your balance was thrown off. So once I had completed the first bar of the step, I lifted my chin back up, and just looked down with my eyes. This really did help, for anyone who has this problem. I was very tall, and when I looked like I was the same height as the other dancers, it was a problem. The dance progressed, my mind didn't drift to other memories as it did in the Fling. I was rather focused. At this moment, I was starting to realise, I had never danced so well. Not just the Swords but today. Entering the last step, slightly into my comfort zone now, I replaced all my body's whining with my last energy stores. As I backstepped out of the Swords, the most worrying part, I kept my focus intact. I've seen people relax prematurely at this stage as they are so close to the end and they have kicked them. Once, I kicked them as I stepped to bow so I was always very cautious of relaxing until those pipes stopped. I stepped to the right, closed my feet and bowed.

As I was standing waiting for the judges to allow me to walk off, I realised something very unexpected. I really was at the top of my game, I was dancing better than ever before and people were actually watching me and cheering. I knew, in that moment that this was the last Swords I would ever do on this stage. I never realised how much this art, this craft, this passion meant to me until that very moment. I felt a tear, slide down my face. As it reached my bib, underneath my jacket, I realised there would come a day that I would regret leaving but you know when you know. This wasn't the first time I had had a thought like this. My mum took me to Toronto, Canada when I was 11 years old. I had said, months before we left, that once Canada was done and we arrived home safely, I would quit Highland Dancing. However, something happened when I was out there. It was the first time, definitely not the last, that I travelled abroad for Dancing. We travelled with our friends from Northern Ireland and other dancers from my school. We were at the pre-championship competition, and I thought that this might be the last time that people saw me dance so I gave it my all. The results came; Fling, nothing. Swords, nothing. Seann Truibhas, nothing. I was feeling downtrodden and then it happened. Half Tullouch, first. It was in that moment I realised I needed to carry on and that wasn't when I was meant to stop dancing. But see, this was different. I was not saying I was never going to dance again, but I knew this would be my last Cowal. No matter the results. And I had never had a sadder moment in my life. The judges nodded, I took a deep breath and after wishing the girl behind me good luck, I walked proudly away from the swords and out into normality once more.

~ 6 ~
Seann Truibhas

The pressure eased slightly that the Swords was over but there was still the nerve of doing something wrong. Making a mistake, or just having a complete brain blank moment and this feeling was enhanced by a previous experience. I had been doing my usual, chatting and warming up beside my fellow competitors. Back then, there was no such thing as nerves at Cowal, I was happy and relaxed. This particular year, we had a leap step. If my memory serves correctly, it was the fourth step. As I finished the movement before, in the space of a few milliseconds, I forgot what step I was going into. I think I was trying to go into the balance step, and when I realised, just-in-time, that I was going onto the wrong step, I threw my foot from fourth intermediate (the corner) to 2nd (straight to the side) and tried to bring my supporting foot up at the same time. I never saw it, but I can imagine it was the weirdest leap in the Highland Dancing history, uneven, unbalanced, and weird. Something cracked, something hurt, and most importantly, I stopped. In Highland Dancing, I rarely stopped. Even when I made a mistake, normally a couple of hops would get you back on time, back into the right position, or the right movement. But this time I had stopped. There was a mixture of I've hurt myself, I've made a mistake, and I am so embarrassed. The embarrassment was the worst part, I limped off of the stage and a massive deal was made by all the judges and officials that were there. It's weird because nobody actually expects a non-champion dancer to get injured. You only ever hear about the champions that injured themselves. I collected myself, and I walked back over to my mum and my sister. The next few weeks, especially that particular day, were filled with comments such as: Nicole why did you pretend to be injured when you just made a mistake, Nicole you're not injured, Nicole, I would never have expected you of all people to get injured. At that moment, I really didn't know if I was hurt, or it was embarrassment or what it was. When we are children, we cry when we fall. Not because it hurts, just because of shock. And I couldn't help but feel that this may be like that.

We jump to a couple of weeks later when I was still moaning about a bit of pain in my calf. Now, whether this injury, if you can call it that had come from a previous injury or because I had tried to go into one step and changed my mind halfway through or if I had just pulled a muscle. However, I had complained enough for mum to take me to my sister's physiotherapist. Nobody believed me there. I had still danced on it but it hurt. Just needed one person to believe me. I got nervous when I entered the physio room, she started going up and down my legs with this vibrating machine and it hurt like 1 million bee stings all at once. I can't remember how long the appointment lasted but it was my only trip to a physio in my life and hopefully the last. I'm sure there probably should've been more. But this was my only one. I think it lasted about 45 minutes to an hour. And by the end of the appointment, we had some answers. It was soft tissue damage in the calf. For anyone who doesn't know what that is, it's not a serious affliction. A soft tissue injury is the damage of muscles, ligaments and tendons throughout the body. Common soft tissue injuries usually occur from a sprain, strain, a one off thing resulting because of an overuse of a particular part of the body, it normally results in pain, swelling, bruising and if left untreated loss of function. Mine was very mild, a minimal overstretch. If left untreated, and if I had continued to dance on it, I would've been unable to apply pressure or weight on my leg without pain - it could've got really bad. Which is why, when you're injured or even a little sore, tell someone and I hope they believe you.

Since this has happened a couple of years prior, I was nervous for this dance. It wasn't that I was scared I was going to spark the same injury again. But what that did teach me, is indecision can sometimes be the most harmful thing you can do to your body. If I had gone into the right step and not second-guessed myself, I might not have got injured. When anybody goes onto a stage to perform, or a gymnasium floor, the need to be 100% ready, prepared, and know what they're doing. I would've actually been better just going into the wrong step, realising I made the mistake, and walking off that year. And if I had got seriously injured, it wouldn't have just been competitions or dance classes that were affected. I took physical education in school, therefore my exams would've been in danger. I walked from school to home and home to school, add a physical job, and I travelled the world dancing. I went to so many different countries, and so many kinds of tattoos, army bases, and amazing shows. It was my life! Dancing was my life. And just because I wasn't a champion winning every competition, didn't mean that I wasn't out there dancing. Maybe more than champion dancers. So if I have got injured, I would've ruined my life as I knew it.

But I knew this year was going to be different, because of my scare, I always made sure I knew every single little thing I was going up there to do. If anything, it had made the Seann Truibhas become one of my best dances. This was the first dance that I didn't feel sorry for myself as I walked up. I stood up there, I looked my judges in the eye, and I was proud. My body had elongated to the height it should be. My jacket had no crease as it was sitting on such a straight specimen. The wind, I could feel, blowing through my kilt and onto my legs and I genuinely felt like I looked majestic. I knew I was going to dance well so as a bowed a smile came across my face. As I rose and stepped to the side my arms came up to 3rd and I looked out into the audience with pride. As I began my first step, I felt the elevation within me explode out. The boards under my feet became a trampoline and every time I jumped I sprang into a new confidence. The first step came to an end and then the second and third and instead of losing energy I was picking energy up from whatever there was around me. The fourth step came and I knew which step, which movements, and what I needed to do. I could feel myself starting to lose energy at the tail end of the fourth step and I started to panic. Then I remembered the clap. The energy drink of movements! That clap was so full of energy, excitement and determination. I clapped. I entered the first last step with an unknown enthusiasm I never knew I possessed. The music was quickening and so was my want to do well. As the last step came upon us, I could actually notice that I was dancing higher, that my technique was brilliant and I quickly gave myself just a second to look at the judges who were all looking at me. All three of them. One of them had a smile of a delighted shock on her face. I think this was the best I had ever danced in my entire life, this one dance was everything! As the end of the dance was looming, I assembled, bent my knees and dug myself into the floorboards just to shoot out both my legs in an explosive movement of power and landed into my future and as I did so - I did not wobble. I did not fall. I stood there for a second proud of what I had just done. I stepped to the side, I closed my feet and I bowed. This may have been the last time I ever done the Seann Truibhas on that stage but it was also the best dance I have ever done in my entire life.

As I walked off of the stage and into the warmup boards, I was out of breath and could barely talk. But even my fellow competitors, the ones who never really saw me as much more than a laugh, they look shocked. And nothing ever brought a smile to my face more than that moment, seeing those reactions. Seeing someone else panic for once as they looked at me like I was a competitor... Finally.

~ 7 ~
Hullachan

I should start by saying that I will be referring to this dance by all of it's formal and informal names in this chapter. Hullachan, Reel, Highland Reel, Strathspey, Half Tulloch and Full Tulloch. This was the only dance, in my opinion, with so many options. Not just with the names but with the steps and performance styles. It was also the only dance in Highland Dancing were you danced with other dancers and not solo, four to be precise. If there wasn't enough people in your group, the first few dancers of the group would have to volunteer. I always found that word funny because none of us were volunteering to dance again – we were told too.

Every dance changed its championship steps every year. But in the Fling you were 99% sure you're going to have to jump on the same spot consistently, do some shedding, some back steps thrown in and probably shove a couple of toe and heels or rocking in there for good measure. The sword dance could change however you were still guaranteed a first step inclusive of 20 pas de basques and 16 highcuts. The only difference being was there could be three slow steps followed by a quick step or two slow steps followed by two quick steps. The latter being the more uncommon choice. So we moved to the Seann Truibhas. This again very expected. First step and second step never really changed much. This particular year, the second step changed ever so slightly for the adults meaning you had to close a foot in front instead of behind. And trust me this was a bigger deal than it sounds. Well to some people. The third and fourth step normally went together quite well, but as I mentioned before that doesn't mean you always remember which one you're doing. Normally, there is a leap thrown in there, normally at least four actually. However, this year was not that year. Everybody was so angry about it because they didn't get to do their prize-winning leaps – that was not me. I loved it. One at the end of the dance, even two was fine for me. The last steps of the Seann Truibhas was very much like plucking two steps out of the Highland Fling throwing them in there and adding a cool ending.

The biggest difference about this year was the choice of Reel/Hullachan – as I said it went by many names. We are used to a strathspey and Highland Reel or a Strathspey and Half Tulloch. But this year I was excited. Not just with this dance but with every single dance. The steps were made for me, the steps were actually steps I was good at. I had been given everything I could have possibly been given to help this year.

In a dance like the Hullachan, there was plenty of time to think about what you needed to do. There was plenty of time to stop and take a breath. And there was plenty of time to be able to face all of the different competitors you were dancing with and feed off the energy they had and dance better.

I loved our Reel. Wasn't a massive fan of strathspeys (too many body angles to account for) and I wasn't a massive fan of highland reeling (too fast and too many people trying to dance into you at all times). Plus, this year the dance had balancing steps, and for someone with long straight lines (most of the time) it was perfect!

Reels seemed to hold the funniest stories. Once when I was doing one at an outdoor competition a wasp followed me from start to finish and I was terrified. I tried to dance and keep my cool whilst the judge could only watch and laugh at the whole situation.

In Musselburgh, not three weeks earlier than Cowal, I was it a major championship called the British Open, ran by my dance teachers. I cannot remember exactly why this particular dancer left the stage on this day, but she left anyway. A mother from a local dance school had jumped into this Reel as you need the four people to dance, but she didn't know what she was doing. I had to fight my way through the rest of my age group that didn't seem to be moving. I got to this dance mother and told her to sit down and I will take it from there. I couldn't dance full-out, because you're not supposed to 'volunteer' before doing your own but I did. I saved the day as some would say, well it's what I said. As I danced, I realised that I only had another set until I was dancing again. You may recall me saying earlier that my fitness was not up to scratch and at this point, I realised I was about to find out how 'not up to scratch' it was. This was actually one of the tougher Championships of the year. People had already started coming over from Australia and America etc to come and complete for Cowal Highland Gathering. This would be a warmup championship for them so I definitely wasn't loving my odds. I had come to this championship with a defeatist attitude and just danced because I was being told to.

As I went out for my Real Reel, as you may say, I was absolutely knackered – Exhausted was probably an understatement. I danced, I felt pretty good about what I had done. By that, I was proud I had got through it without collapsing, but it did help that there had been zero pressure. At this championship, like a few others, they did the highland results before we went further – into more dances. Well, they did back when I danced. Truthfully everything I am saying could have changed by now. Based on the art form being based fully on tradition, I can't imagine there being too many differences. My jacket was off, I was drinking Irn-Bru, and I was watching the results out of interest. I didn't even know my number on my kilt to be called if I was. So the Fling result came, nothing. The Swords - nothing. Then Seann Truibhas - nothing. This was normal for me. I wasn't mad or angry or jealous! I used to have a lot of these emotions many years previous but none at this point. I had accepted my fate as a dancer a long time ago. Then the Reel results came in, and one of my best friends got first. Then second, third and fourth. Then something rather strange and unexpected happened.

I got fifth!

Not even sixth... Fifth! Everybody was so excited and stared at me aghast. It took me a minute before I realised what had happened whilst more and more people started staring at me. I could see the dancers in the line-up and even they were staring now. Then it hit me. I jumped up and had to run, a run that everybody hated watching. They normally get annoyed but not today. There wore a few cheers – nobody got cheers for a random fifth in a random dance. Not only was I running but I was having to do up a jacket of which the buttons were being very uncooperative. I swear I thought I was the best dancer in the world at that point. I took the prize money and stood in line in between all the dancers that I saw up here all of the time. But my friend, who had got first, and I didn't leave the stage after the Reel result. We had looked at each other and I stopped the tears falling. At that moment, she ran up to me and hugged me saying well done, I am so proud of you. I didn't hold the tears back for very long during that. It was a moment in dancing that I realised that a fifth to some people meant more than winning to others. I pulled away from the hug that nobody interrupted and looked up to everybody clapping and cheering – Real sportsmanship was hard to find in any sport but this was a true moment. All twelve judges looked at me and realised the same thing – how truly thankful I was. It was one of the best days of my Highland Dancing life. I had always been as supportive as I possibly could be to all of my friends, most of which were champions. I never complained to them that I should have done better or that I was sad that I didn't get a placing. I was never ungrateful. Which meant getting a fifth at one of the biggest championships of the year was the greatest feeling and to get love from my fellow dancer showed me they cared too.

This championship was run by my amazing dance teachers. And when it came to running something like this, it obviously took a lot of clean-up at the end of the weekend. So we were all helping tidy up and one of my dance teachers asked me to take something, or a few somethings, out to her car. I happily agreed as I was still on cloud nine. So she gave me her keys and I headed out with a handful of stuff. Walking as you do when your mum asks you to help her take the shopping out of the car and you try to take it all at once. I just finished putting everything in the car, with a smile still burning my face, and I heard it. A group of grown women talking about the only reason that I had got the placing. They said that because I jumped in for the Reel before I danced, the judges may have gone easier on me and placed me because of it. I had hid behind the car and continued to listen as they laughed at the thought of me getting placed. I cried softly in that spot for five minutes and let the group disperse. Once they were gone, I had cleaned myself of and walked back in to help tidy up after everyone.

There will always be negativity and we all know we should just listen to the positivity. But I didn't realise that straightaway as most of us don't. I cried myself to sleep that night thinking I wasn't good enough. I had always strived to be nice to everybody my entire life. All I ever wanted was people to like me and have people laugh at something I said, not at my achievements. I just wanted people to love me. People spoke like this about a teenager and I cry now thinking about how awful I felt. I kept thinking that I had to be thankful for them bringing me back to reality. That was actually why I was trying so hard at Cowal, just so nobody could say that again – that I didn't deserve it. My dance teachers always told me I should always maintain good sportsmanship and my mum and dad always told me to be nice. I also had a sister who provided me with a fantastic example. She was graceful in victory and defeat. I'm so glad I heard what they said because when I thought about that just before I went up for this Reel, I got a rage deep down inside of me – in my heart and soul. To this day, I don't think they ever thought I heard them, and I probably shouldn't remember it but I still occasionally think of it to this day. Sadly, you will probably remember the bad things that happen more than the good things which is a shame because in the good times, Highland Dancing made you feel like you were on top of the world. But please if you plan to say something cold or judgemental about people or make your own little comments, at least look round the corner or wait until you're in your car. Don't take the joy from somebody. It can be the most exciting thing in the world for someone to get a fifth, a sixth or even a championship point. For context, a championship point is when one or more of the three judges had placed you, but you didn't quite get enough points to get a placing. There are people out there getting their championship point once in a lifetime, and they can sometimes be more excited than someone winning their hundredth championship. Please do not take this away from them. It is literally all we hang onto when it comes to these hard Championships. If you start to hear comments like this and want to quit, I can tell you right now - those people aren't worth it. I Promise. Do not quit because of them. There is only one word for it. Jealousy. If I had quit then, I would have missed the most successful year of my Highland Dancing life. I kept dancing in spite of the comments. Due to social media and the world being a lot smaller than you think. I have to see some of these people occasionally. Every time I see them, I do remember and sadden. However, I have got a reputation now of being quite a funny, happy person so I hide it and talk to them forever thinking of the day I become successful and can finally tell myself it was because I was good enough. Through life you will go through times where you are successful and other times you definitely fail but each decision, good or bad, takes you where you need to be.

~ 9 ~
The Results

Results were different at every competition. Not only the way they did them but the dancers that got first in every competition may not even get placed somewhere like this. This championship was huge and everybody was there that day.

Any athlete, dancer or sportsperson will tell you that some results and some competitions you will never forget. Results wise, there were only a few for me but I still call them some of the happiest days of my life.

There was a competition in a small fishing town named Oban. They were one of the few places that were not bogged down with traditional dances but unique choreographies made by our own dance teachers. I absolutely loved it! We did it for years and we got placings. I can't remember them all but off the top of my mind, I had been dressed as a witch, a farmer, a fisherman, a shot putter and so many more crazy characters. One year, we did a dance based on my favourite magical author and the masterpiece she created. All the dancers had sat in a circle and decided to discuss which character we were all going to play. My sister knew exactly who I wanted and knew I wouldn't say it myself, so she spoke up for me. Nobody disagreed so I took that as I would get to play a specky boy wizard and I have never been happier with a casting choice. My sister got to play my bushy haired best friend which didn't take much preparation with her thick, curly, natural hair. It was the hardest I have ever worked so when we danced it, it was spectacular. All of us came together with ideas and it was amazing.

We were sitting in the crowd after dancing waiting for results and the hall was a buzz of excitement and anticipation. At this competition they announced the results backwards, from 6th to 1st and I loved the build up. All the places were coming and we still hadn't been called. I was deflated to say the least. And then, they said first… Our dance school. I was the first on my feet running to the stage as I had never got first in Oban before in my life. I walked up and retrieved my prize with the rest of my school not long behind. I was shaking, crying –

basically an emotional wreck. This is how Charlene must have felt all the time when she won. Our dance teachers came up on the stage and one stood at each side of their twelve hard working, committed dancers. It was only then that I was reminded, we would have to re-dance due to us winning. I had no idea how I was going to do it with my body shaking. That winning dance is how I imagine the world champions feel when they have to do the same thing at Cowal Highland Gathering.

However, the best moment that actually tops every single one I ever talk about would be on October 3rd 2010, when I was just 13 years old in the age group of 13 - 15 years being one of the youngest in my group. This was a Pre-Championship. Only people that had never won one before and had never won a championship could compete in a competition like this. By this time, I had been competing for this win for 4 years and it was beginning to get frustrating with how close I had been so many times, and yet so far. Anybody that was there that day will attest to the reactions and the atmosphere in that hall. Let me explain:

We were in Dumfries at one of the last championships of the year. It was a nice day, the sun was out but a small autumn breeze was definitely apparent. My Northern Irish friend and I were both set to dance. The days started with the age groups getting all mixed up. We were meant to be dancing in the age group and if we had, things could have turned out very differently. She ended up being in the younger group and as I stated earlier, I ended up being in the 15 years and under at only 13 years old, making me one of the youngest in the group. Nerves had long left me, after doing something for so many years, you grew accustomed to what you had to do and how to go about it. I guess you could say, it was like riding a bike and I had chopped my stabilizers off a long time ago. I danced as I danced every competition, well apparently better than most. The results came for my friend first. As I saw her win dance after dance, I knew that her dream had come true and soon she would have a new one. She had won her pre championships! It had deflated me slightly, as I still hadn't had my results yet and didn't know how I had done. Then they came.

First result, the Fling, and it wasn't quite what we were looking for but still good. 5th. As we bowed and I slowly walked off the stage, I heard the second result (the Swords). I had got first. With a slight enthusiasm this time, I took my prize and bowed. Heading off again, the third dance, the Seann Truibhas... Second! Now due to the mixed results, I had no idea how I had done overall. By this point the hall was starting to fill with people getting ready for their championship in the afternoon. I looked over to my sister, my mum, and two dance teachers to get any hint of how I was doing. But they were all looking down. Later I realised they were trying to quickly add up all the points and find out what I needed to win. Apparently, my sister had turned round and said, she just needs to beat that one girl and she's got it – Unfortunately, Charlene was not aware of the girl's family sitting behind her. That still brings a smile to my face. And here it was, the Reel. Those few seconds in between the bow from the last result and the next, seemed to last minutes. And then I heard it. I had got first!

I walked up, still unsure of if I had won or not and bowed. As I walked towards my family, I could tell by their faces that I had done it. I could tell I had won. Now this didn't happen at many competitions, but at this particular one they didn't wait until the end to give out the trophies. They gave them out after each group so before I could do anything, all I heard was 15 years and under Pre-Championship winner - Nicole McMahon. I can still hear the cheer that I got to this day.

This massive hall had erupted!

I burst into tears if joy! Every single eye in the hall was on me and even the judges looked so happy for me. I still don't understand why everyone was so loud but I loved it! It was the best moment of my life as I walked back, trophy in hand. I could barely even get to my sister, mum or dance teachers to give them a cuddle because a queue had formed as long as the hall of dancers, parents, teachers and judges, that just wanted to say well done. I know a lot of people reading this, will think that I am exaggerating. But there was actually a queue! I had never felt so loved, appreciated or amazing in my entire life.

Back to Cowal though, I sure can get off track! Here, they called all the numbers that had been placed in numerical order as the stage was so far away from the seating area. I normally got out of my kilt and into my normal clothes before the numbers even came out due to lack of confidence and it had always served me well but this time, I didn't. My age group was announced and they began reading out the numbers. When they were still lower than my number, there was a tension in my body as I said my number over and over again in my mind whilst trying to remain cool, calm and collected. It was getting closer and my body was getting stiffer and stiffer as my number was on the approach. The tension that could only be replaced by relief or disappointment. They said the number before me. It was now or never. And then…

They said the number after mine. I hadn't got placed. Mum always gave me this look of reassurance but I really think this time, she thought I was going to get placed. For one of the few times in my dancing career, I felt an overwhelming feeling of despair. I had tried so hard and this had been my last chance to prove I could do it. I was absolutely gutted and for once I didn't know what to do and I didn't know what to say. I looked into my mum's eyes and I think she knew what I was feeling. We knew better than acting on these feelings right then in front of everyone. So, we pretended everything was fine. She continued writing results and as I had watched, I got changed out of my kilt for the last time at Cowal Highland Gathering. I would love to say that everyone always gets their time but it just didn't happen, I had been dancing there for 8 years and had 15 chances but nothing. I had never got anything. I put a smile on my face as we collected our belongings and headed for our temporary home.

At the end of the results, pieces of paper were put up that showed exactly what each judge had picked for their 1st − 6th in each dance. It was always an interesting read. I felt numb as I walked with my head down, hoping nobody would speak to me. I had felt someone running towards me so I looked up and saw my dancing friend. She was shouting my name over and over again and passed the results sheet to my mum who read. She looked at me with an amazing awe-struck look but no words seemed to come out of any of their mouths. I snatched the sheet from mum and looked down. Highland Fling, judge one, I looked at their line-up and then I saw it my number written beside 5th. I frantically asked my mum if that was my number and she was nodding. I couldn't hold it anymore and burst into tears. It took all my energy to stay standing. I hugged absolutely everyone that was in reach, I was so extatically happy that I had no idea what to do. And even though I was terrified somebody was going to tell me that I hadn't deserved the result, I didn't care. I knew I did and I knew nobody would have been as happy as me. I was going out on a high. One judge thought, on that day, I was the 5th best in Scotland at the Highland Fling.

~ The End ~

(And possibly also, the beginning...?)

Printed in Great Britain
by Amazon

76904071R00051